W9-BFN-467

Further Fables for Our Time

by
JAMES THURBER

Illustrated by the Author

SIMON AND SCHUSTER
New York

COPYRIGHT © 1956 BY JAMES THURBER
ALL RIGHTS RESERVED
INCLUDING THE RIGHT OF REPRODUCTION
IN WHOLE OR IN PART IN ANY FORM
PUBLISHED BY SIMON AND SCHUSTER
A DIVISION OF GULF & WESTERN CORPORATION
SIMON & SCHUSTER BUILDING
ROCKEFELLER CENTER
1230 AVENUE OF THE AMERICAS
NEW YORK, NEW YORK 10020

MANUFACTURED IN THE UNITED STATES OF AMERICA

1   2   3   4   5   6   7   8   9   10

Library of Congress Cataloging in Publication Data

Thurber, James, 1894-1961
  Further fables for our time.

  (A Fireside book)
  1.   Fables, American.   I.   Title.
PS3539.H94F8   1978   818'.5'207   77-26827
ISBN 0-671-27880-0
ISBN 0-671-24218-0 Pbk.

TO ELMER DAVIS

whose comprehension of people and persons
has lighted our time, so that we can see where
we are going, these fables are dedicated with
admiration, affection, and thankfulness

ACKNOWLEDGMENT

Thirty-seven of these fables originally appeared in *The New Yorker*, but these ten are printed here for the first time:

The Sea and the Shore, The Lion and the Foxes, The Hen Party, The Bears and the Monkeys, The Chipmunk and His Mate, The Trial of the Old Watchdog, The Godfather and His Godchild, Tea for One, The Lady of the Legs and *The Shore and the Sea.*

CONTENTS

ix

The Sea
and the Shore

A PAIR of gibbous creatures, who had lived in the sea since time began, which hadn't been long before, were washed upon the shore one day and became the discoverers of land. "The light that never was!" exclaimed the female, lying on the sand in the sun.

"You're always seeing things that never were," grumbled the male. "You're always wanting things that aren't yet."

In the female, lying on the sand in the sun, a dim intuition and prescience began developing. She prefigured mistily things that would one day become rose-point lace and taffeta, sweet perfumes and jewelry. The male, who had a feeling only for wetness and wash, mumbled, "You're a little moist for things like that, a little moist and shapeless."

"I only need to lose a little amorphousness around the waist," she said. "It won't take more than a million years." And she began flobbering, almost imperceptibly, toward the scrubby brown growth beyond the sand and toward the sun. "Come on," she said. But the male had globbed back into the sea, and was gone.

A couple of eons later, the male, unable to get along alone, reappeared one day upon the shore. He noted with faint satisfaction that the female's shapelessness was beginning to take shape and had become almost shapely. He turned back toward the sea, but a mindless urge deep inside him took on the frail flicker of desire. Suddenly the sea seemed something less than satisfying. He turned about and began flobbering up the sand toward the female, who seemed certain to reach the greening undergrowth in another two thousand years. "Hey, Mag," he shouted. "Wait for baby!"

MORAL: *Let us ponder this basic fact about the human: Ahead of every man, not behind him, is a woman.*

The Truth About Toads

ONE MIDSUMMER NIGHT at the Fauna Club, some of the members fell to boasting, each of his own unique distinction or achievement.

"I am the real Macaw," squawked the Macaw proudly.

"O.K., Mac, take it easy," said the Raven, who was tending bar.

"You should have seen the one I got away from," said the Marlin. "He must have weighed a good two hundred and thirty-five pounds."

"If it weren't for me, the sun would never rise," bragged the Rooster, "and the desire of the night for the morrow would never be gratified." He wiped a tear away. "If it weren't for me, nobody would get up."

"If it weren't for me, there wouldn't *be* anybody," the Stork reminded him proudly.

"I tell them when spring is coming," the Robin chirped.

"I tell them when winter will end," the Groundhog said.

"I tell them how deep the winter will be," said the Woolly Bear.

"I swing low when a storm is coming," said the Spider. "Otherwise it wouldn't come, and the people would die of a drought."

The Mouse got into the act. "You know where it says, 'Not a creature was stirring, not even a mouse'?" he hiccuped. "Well, gentlemen, that little old mouse was little old me."

"Quiet!" said the Raven, who had been lettering a sign and now hung it prominently above the bar: "Open most hearts and you will see graven upon them Vanity."

The members of the Fauna Club stared at the sign. "Probably means the Wolf, who thinks he founded Rome," said the Cat.

"Or the great Bear, who thinks he is made of stars," said the Mouse.

"Or the golden Eagle, who thinks he's made of gold," said the Rooster.

"Or the Sheep, who thinks men couldn't sleep unless they counted sheep," said the Marlin.

The Toad came up to the bar and ordered a green mint frappé with a firefly in it.

"Fireflies will make you lightheaded," warned the bartender.

"Not me," said the Toad. "Nothing can make me lightheaded. I have a precious jewel in my head." The other members of the club looked at him with mingled disbelief.

"Sure, sure," grinned the bartender, "It's a toadpaz, ain't it, Hoppy?"

"It is an extremely beautiful emerald," said the Toad coldly, removing the firefly from his frappé and swallowing it. "Absolutely priceless emerald. *More* than priceless. Keep 'em comin'. "

The bartender mixed another green mint frappé, but he put a slug in it this time instead of a firefly.

"I don't think the Toad has a precious jewel in his head," said the Macaw.

"I do," said the Cat. "Nobody could be that ugly and live unless he had an emerald in his head."

"I'll bet you a hundred fish he hasn't," said the Pelican.

"I'll bet you a hundred clams he has," said the Sandpiper.

The Toad, who was pretty well frappéd by

this time, fell asleep, and the members of the club debated how to find out whether his head held an emerald, or some other precious stone. They summoned the Woodpecker from the back room and explained what was up. "If he hasn't got a hole in his head, I'll make one," said the Woodpecker.

There wasn't anything there, gleaming or lovely or precious. The bartender turned out the lights, the Rooster crowed, the sun came up, and the members of the Fauna Club went silently home to bed.

MORAL: *Open most heads and you will find nothing shining, not even a mind.*

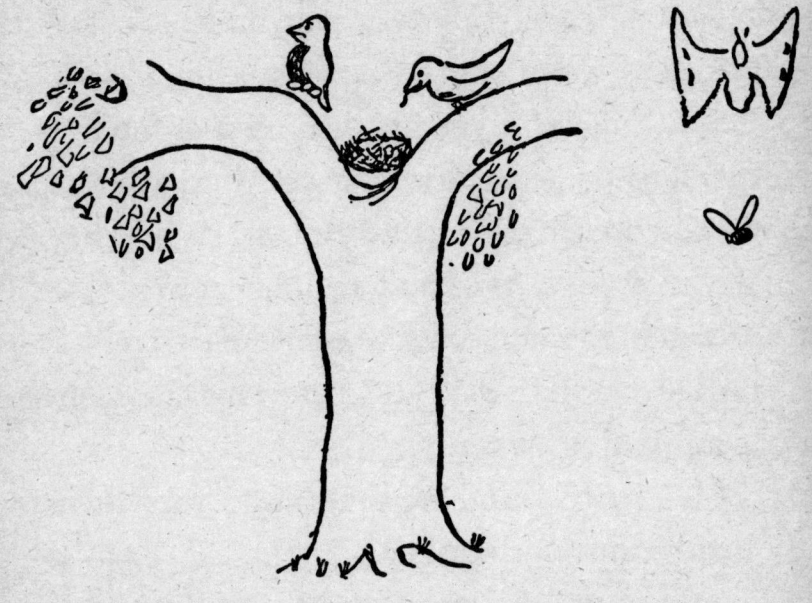

The Butterfly,
the Ladybug,
and the Phoebe

A PHOEBE, bugwinner for a nestful of fledglings, flew out one day to provide dinner for his family, and came upon a ladybug in frantic flight.

"I know you can catch anything smaller than a golf ball and slower than sound," said the ladybug, "for you are the fastest of the fly-catchers, but my house is on fire and my children will burn unless I fly away home."

The phoebe, who had sometimes been guilty of wishing that his own house were on fire, let the ladybug fly away, and turned his attention to a beautiful butterfly.

"Is your house on fire and will your children burn?" the phoebe asked.

"Nothing so mundane as all that," said the butterfly. "I have no children and I have no house, for I am an angel, as anyone can see." She fluttered her wings at the world about her. "This is heaven," she said.

"This is heaven," cried the fledglings, as one fledgling, when they had the butterfly for dessert that night.

MORAL: *She who goes unarmed in Paradise should first be sure that's where she is.*

The Foolhardy Mouse
and the Cautious Cat

SUCH SPORT there had been that day, in the kitchen and the pantry, for the cat was away and the mice were playing all manner of games: mousy-wants-a-corner, hide-and-squeak, one-old-cat, mouse-in-boots, and so on. Then the cat came home.

"Cat's back!" whispered Father Mouse.

"Into the wainscoting, all of you!" said Mother Mouse, and all of the mice except one hastily hid in the woodwork.

The exception was an eccentric mouse named Mervyn, who had once boldly nipped a bulldog in the ear and got away with it. Mervyn did not know at the time, and never found out, that the bulldog was a stuffed bulldog, and so he lived in a fool's paradise.

The day the cat, whose name was Pouncetta, came back from wherever she had been, she was astonished to encounter Mervyn in the butler's pantry, nonchalantly nibbling crumbs. She crept toward him in her stocking feet and was astounded when he turned, spit a crumb in her eye, and began insulting her with a series of insults.

"How did you get out of the bag?" Mervyn inquired calmly. "Put on your pajamas and take a cat nap." He went back to his nibbling, as blasé as you please.

"Steady, Pouncetta," said Pouncetta to herself. "There is more here than meets the eye. This mouse is probably a martyr mouse. He has swallowed poison in the hope that I will eat him and die, so that he can be a hero to a hundred generations of his descendants."

Mervyn looked over his shoulder at the startled and suspicious cat and began to mock her in a mousetto voice. "Doodness dwacious," said Mervyn, "it's a posse cat, in full pursuit of little me." He gestured impudently with one foot. "I went that-a-way," he told Pouncetta. Then he did some other imitations, including a pretty good one of W. C. Fieldmouse.

"Easy, girl," said Pouncetta to herself. "This is a mechanical mouse, a trick mouse with a built-in voice. If I jump on it, it will explode and blow me into a hundred pieces. Damned clever, these mice, but not clever enough for me."

"You'd make wonderful violin strings, if you had any guts," Mervyn said insolently. But Pouncetta did not pounce, in spite of the insult unforgivable. Instead, she turned and stalked out of the butler's pantry and into the sitting room and lay down on her pillow near the fireplace and went to sleep.

When Mervyn got back to his home in the

woodwork, his father and mother and brothers and sisters and cousins and uncles and aunts were surprised to see him alive and well. There was great jollity, and the finest cheese was served at a family banquet. "She never laid a paw on me," Mervyn boasted. "I haven't got a scratch. I could take on all the cats in the Catskills." He finished his cheese and went to bed and fell asleep, and dreamed of taking a catamount in one minute and twenty-eight seconds of the first round.

MORAL: *Fools rush in where angels fear to tread, and the angels are all in Heaven, but few of the fools are dead.*

The Rose
and the Weed

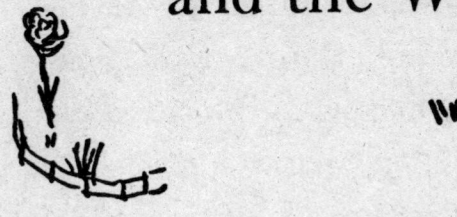

IN A COUNTRY GARDEN a lovely rose looked down upon a common weed and said, "You are an unwelcome guest, economically useless, and unsightly of appearance. The Devil must love weeds, he made so many of them."

The unwelcome guest looked up at the rose and said, "Lilies that fester smell far worse than weeds, and, one supposes, that goes for roses."

"My name is Dorothy Perkins," the rose said haughtily. "What are you—a beetleweed, a bladderweed, a beggarweed? The names of weeds are ugly." And Dorothy shuddered slightly, but lost none of her pretty petals.

"We have some names prettier than Perkins, or, for my taste, Dorothy, among them silverweed, and jewelweed, and candyweed." The weed straightened a bit and held his ground. "Anywhere you can grow I can grow better," he said.

"I think you must be a burglarweed," said the disdainful Miss Perkins, "for you get in where you aren't wanted, and take what isn't yours—the rain and the sunlight and the good earth."

The weed smiled a weedy smile. "At least," he said, "I do not come from a family of climbers."

The rose drew herself up to her full height. "I'd have you know that roses are the emblem of old England," she said. "We are the flower of song and story."

"And of war," the weed replied. "The summer winds take you by storm, not you the winds with beauty. I've seen it happen many times, to roses of yesteryear, long gone and long forgotten."

"We are mentioned in Shakespeare," said the rose, "many times in many plays. The lines are too sweet for your ears, but I will tell you some."

Just then, and before Miss Perkins could recite, a wind came out of the west, riding low to the ground and swift, like the cavalry of March, and Dorothy Perkins' beautiful disdain suddenly became a scattering of petals, economically useless, and of appearance not especially sightly. The weed stood firm, his head to the wind, armored, or so he thought, in security and strength, but as he was brushing a few rose petals and aphids from his lapels, the hand of the gardener flashed out of the air and pulled him out of the ground by the roots before you could say Dorothy Perkins, or, for that matter, jewelweed.

MORAL: Tout, *as the French say, in a philosophy older than ours and an idiom often more succinct,* passe.

The Bat Who Got the Hell Out

A COLONY of bats living in a great American cave had got along fine for a thousand generations, flying, hanging head down, eating insects, and raising young, and then one year a male named Flitter, who had fluttered secretly out of his room at night and flown among the haunts of men, told his father that he had decided to get the hell out. The shocked father sent Flitter to Fleder, the great-great-grandfather of all the bats in the cave.

he could say, "You have no more soul than a moose, or a mouse, or a mole. You should be glad that you will never become an angel, for angels do not have true flight. One wants to *sleep* through eternity, not bumble and flap about forever like a bee or a butterfly."

But Flitter had made up his mind, and the old bat's words of wisdom were in vain. That night, the discontented young bat quit the bat colony, and flickered out of the cave, in the confident hope of giving up his membership in the Chiroptera and joining the happy breed of men. Unfortunately for his dream, he spent his first night hanging head down from the rafters of an auditorium in which a best-selling Inspirationalist was dragging God down to the people's level. Ushers moved silently among the rapt listeners, selling copies of the speaker's books: *Shake Hands with the Almighty, You Can Be Jehovah's Pal* and *Have You Taken Out Eternity Insurance?* The speaker was saying, "Have a little talk with the Lord while you're waiting for a bus, or riding to work, or sitting in the dentist's chair. Have comfy chats with the Lord in the little cozy corners of spare time."

Flitter decided that there was something the matter with the acoustics, or with his tragus, caused by hanging head down in the presence of the Eternal Species, but when he began flying about the auditorium, there was no change in the nature of the English sentences. "Tell the Lord to put it there," the inspired man went on. "Give him your duke." The speaker waved clasped hands above his head and gazed up at the ceiling. "Keep pitching, God," he said. "You've got two strikes on Satan."

Flitter, who had never felt sick before in his life, felt sick, and decided to get the air. After he had got the air, he realized that he did not want to become a member of the species *Homo sapiens,* because of the danger of bumbling or flapping into the Inspirationalist after they had both become angels. And so Flitter returned to the cave, and everybody was astonished to see him, and nobody said anything, and for a time there was a great silence.

"I've come the hell back," said Flitter, meekly. And he resumed, without discontent, the immemorial life of the Chiroptera, flying, hanging head down, eating insects, and raising young.

MORAL: *By decent minds is he abhorred who'd make a Babbitt of the Lord.*

The Lion
and the Foxes

THE LION had just explained to the cow,
the goat, and the sheep that the stag they
had killed belonged to him, when three little
foxes appeared on the scene.

"I will take a third of the stag as a penalty,"

said one, "for you have no hunter's license."

"I will take a third of the stag for your widow," said another, "for that is the law."

"I have no widow," said the lion.

"Let us not split hairs," said the third fox, and he took his share of the stag as a withholding tax. "Against a year of famine," he explained.

"But I am king of beasts," roared the lion.

"Ah, then you will not need the antlers, for you have a crown," said the foxes, and they took the antlers, too.

MORAL: *It is not as easy to get the lion's share nowadays as it used to be.*

The Wolf
Who Went Places

A WEALTHY young wolf, who was oblivious of everything except himself, was tossed out of college for cutting classes and corners, and he decided to see if he could travel around the world in eighty minutes.

"That isn't possible," his grandmother told him, but he only grinned at her.

"The impossible is the most fun," he said.

She went with him to the door of the old Wolf place. "If you go that fast, you won't live to regret it," she warned him, but he grinned again, showing a tongue as long as a necktie.

"That's an old wolves' tale," he said, and went on his reckless way.

He bought a 1959 Blitzen Bearcat, a combination motorcar and airplane, with skyrocket getaway, cyclone speedrive, cannonball takeoff, blindall headlights, magical retractable monowings, and lightning pushbutton transformationizer. "How fast can this crate go without burning up?" he asked the Blitzen Bearcat salesman.

"I don't know," the salesman said, "but I have a feeling you'll find out."

The wealthy young wolf smashed all the ground records and air records and a lot of other things in his trip around the world, which took him only 78.5 minutes from the time he knocked down the Washington Monument on his takeoff to the time he landed where it had stood. In the crowd that welcomed him home, consisting of about eleven creatures, for all the others were hiding under beds, there was a speed-crazy young wolfess, with built-in instantaneous pickup ability, and in no time at all the wolf and his new-found mate were setting new records for driving upside down, backward, blindfolded, handcuffed, and cockeyed, doubled and redoubled.

One day, they decided to see if they could turn in to Central Park from Fifth Avenue while traveling at a rate of 175 miles an hour, watching television, and holding hands. There was a tremendous shattering, crashing, splitting, roaring, blazing, cracking, and smashing, ending in a fiery display of wheels, stars, cornices, roofs, treetops, glass, steel, and people, and it seemed to those spectators who did not die of seizures as they watched that great red portals opened in the sky, swinging inward on mighty hinges, revealing an endless nowhere, and then closed behind the flying and flaming wolves with a clanking to end all clanking, as if those gates which we have been assured shall not prevail had, in fact, prevailed.

MORAL: *Where most of us end up there is no knowing, but the hellbent get where they are going.*

The Bluebird
and His Brother

IT WAS SAID of two bluebirds that they were unlike as two brothers could be, that one was a pearl in a pod and the other a pea. Pearl was happy-go-lucky, and Pea was gloomy-go-sorry.

"I am in love with love and life," sang the glad bird.

"I am afraid of sex and flight," sang the sad bird.

Pearl flaunted his gay colors like a bonnie blue flag, and his song was as bold as the Rebel yell. He went South every winter alone, and came North every spring with a different female. His gay philosophy freed his psyche of the stains of fear and the stresses of guilt, and he attained a serenity of spirit that few male birds and even fewer male human beings ever reach. He did not worry because some of his children were also his nieces, the daughters of one of his sisters. He sat loose, sang pretty, and slept tight, in a hundred honey locusts and cherry trees and lilac bushes. And every winter he went South alone, and every spring he came North with a different female. He did not worry because some of his grandchildren were also his grandnephews, the grandsons of one of his sisters.

At sunset in summertime, the gay bluebird flew higher than the lark or the wild goose, and he was pleased to note that, like himself, heaven wore blue, with a tinge of red.

The gloomy bluebird went South alone in the winter and came North alone in the spring, and never flew higher than you could throw a sofa. While still in his prime he developed agoraphobia and went to live underground, to the surprise and dismay of families of frogs and foxes and moles and gophers and crickets and toads, and of the bewildered dog who dug him up one day while burying a bone, and then hastily buried him again, without ceremony or sorrow.

MORAL: *It is more dangerous to straight-arm life than to embrace it.*

The Clothes Moth
and the Luna Moth

A CLOTHES MOTH who lived in a closet and had never done anything, or wanted to do anything, except eat wool and fur, flew out of his closet one twilight just in time to see a lovely Luna moth appear on the outside of a windowpane. The Luna moth fluttered against the lighted glass as gracefully as a drifting autumn leaf, and she was dressed in a charming evening gown. What interested her was the flame of a candle burning in the room, burning on the mantelpiece above the fireplace, but the clothes moth thought she was making signs at him, and he conceived a great desire for her.

"I have to have you," said the clothes moth, but the Luna moth laughed, and her laughter was like the bells of elfland faintly tinkling.

"Go eat a shroud," said the Luna moth haughtily. "You are as vulgar as a tent moth, or a gypsy moth, and nowhere near as handsome as a tiger moth."

"If you come to live with me I will feed you on sweaters and stoles," said the clothes moth, whose ardor was only increased by the lovely Luna's scorn.

"You are a flug, who can flugger, but not fly or flutter," said the Luna moth, trying to get through the windowpane and reach the star on the mantelpiece.

"You can have wedding dresses and evening clothes and a mink coat," panted the clothes moth, and again the Luna moth's laughter was like the bells of elfland faintly tinkling.

"I live on twilight and the stars," she said.

"It was love at first flight," the clothes moth protested. "It was love at first flutter."

The Luna moth's tiny silvery tone became sharper. "You are a mulch," she said, "a mulbus, a crawg, and a common creeb."

All these words were words a nice moth rarely uses, but they had no effect upon the passion of the clothes moth.

"I know you have one wing in the grave," he told her. "I know you're not long for this world, and so I must have you as soon as I can. A thing of beauty is a joy for such a little time."

The lovely Luna moth tried to cajole her admirer into opening the window—so that she could fly to the fascinating flame above the fireplace, but she did not tell him this. She let him believe that his drab gray lovemaking had won her heart. In his desire to reach her, he flew against the windowpane time and time again, and finally made a small opening in it, and then fluggered crazily to the floor, dead of a broken head and wings and body. The lovely Luna, whose desire for the star is a matter of immortal record, flew swiftly and gracefully toward the candle on the mantelpiece and was consumed in its flame with a little zishing sound like that made by a lighted cigarette dropped in a cup of coffee.

MORAL: *Love is blind, but desire just doesn't give a good goddam.*

The Lover
and His Lass

An arrogant gray parrot and his arrogant mate listened, one African afternoon, in disdain and derision, to the lovemaking of a lover and his lass, who happened to be hippopotamuses.

"He calls her snooky-ookums," said Mrs. Gray. "Can you believe that?"

"No," said Gray. "I don't see how any male in his right mind could entertain affection for a female that has no more charm than a capsized bathtub."

"Capsized bathtub, indeed!" exclaimed Mrs. Gray. "Both of them have the appeal of a coastwise fruit steamer with a cargo of waterlogged basketballs."

But it was spring, and the lover and his lass were young, and they were oblivious of the scornful comments of their sharp-tongued neighbors, and they continued to bump each other around in the water, happily pushing

and pulling, backing and filling, and snorting and snaffling. The tender things they said to each other during the monolithic give-and-take of their courtship sounded as lyric to them as flowers in bud or green things opening. To the Grays, however, the bumbling romp of the lover and his lass was hard to comprehend and even harder to tolerate, and for a time they thought of calling the A.B.I., or African Bureau of Investigation, on the ground that monolithic lovemaking by enormous creatures who should have become decent fossils long ago was probably a threat to the security of the jungle. But they decided instead to phone their friends and neighbors and gossip about the shameless pair, and describe them in mocking and monstrous metaphors involving skidding buses on icy streets and overturned moving vans.

Late that evening, the hippopotamus and the hippopotama were surprised and shocked to hear the Grays exchanging terms of endearment. "Listen to those squawks," wuffled the male hippopotamus.

"What in the world can they see in each other?" gurbled the female hippopotamus.

"I would as soon live with a pair of unoiled garden shears," said her inamoratus.

They called up their friends and neighbors and discussed the incredible fact that a male gray parrot and a female gray parrot could possibly have any sex appeal. It was long after midnight before the hippopotamuses stopped criticizing the Grays and fell asleep, and the Grays stopped maligning the hippopotamuses and retired to their beds.

MORAL: *Laugh and the world laughs with you, love and you love alone.*

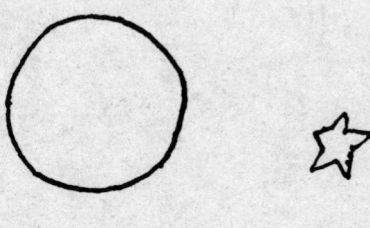

The Fox
and the Crow

A CROW, perched in a tree with a piece of cheese in his beak, attracted the eye and nose of a fox. "If you can sing as prettily as you sit," said the fox, "then you are the prettiest singer within my scent and sight." The fox had read somewhere, and somewhere, and somewhere else, that praising the voice of a crow with a cheese in his beak would make him drop the cheese and sing. But this is not what happened to this particular crow in this particular case.

"They say you are sly and they say you are crazy," said the crow, having carefully removed the cheese from his beak with the claws of one foot, "but you must be nearsighted as well. Warblers wear gay hats and colored jackets and bright vests, and they are a dollar a hundred. I wear black and I am unique." He began nibbling the cheese, dropping not a single crumb.

"I am sure you are," said the fox, who was neither crazy nor nearsighted, but sly. "I recognize you, now that I look more closely, as the most famed and talented of all birds, and I fain would hear you tell about yourself, but I am hungry and must go."

"Tarry awhile," said the crow quickly, "and

share my lunch with me." Whereupon he tossed the cunning fox the lion's share of the cheese, and began to tell about himself. "A ship that sails without a crow's nest sails to doom," he said. "Bars may come and bars may go, but crow bars last forever. I am the pioneer of flight, I am the map maker. Last, but never least, my flight is known to scientists and engineers, geometrists and scholars, as the shortest distance between two points. Any two points," he concluded arrogantly.

"Oh, every two points, I am sure," said the fox. "And thank you for the lion's share of what I know you could not spare." And with this he trotted away into the woods, his appetite appeased, leaving the hungry crow perched forlornly in the tree.

MORAL: *'Twas true in Aesop's time, and La Fontaine's, and now, no one else can praise thee quite so well as thou.*

Variations on the Theme

I

A FOX, attracted by the scent of something, followed his nose to a tree in which sat a crow with a piece of cheese in his beak. "Oh, cheese," said the fox scornfully. "That's for mice."

The crow removed the cheese with his talons and said, "You always hate the thing you cannot have, as, for instance, grapes."

"Grapes are for the birds," said the fox haughtily. "I am an epicure, a gourmet, and a gastronome."

The embarrassed crow, ashamed to be seen eating mouse food by a great specialist in the art of dining, hastily dropped the cheese. The fox caught it deftly, swallowed it with relish, said "*Merci*," politely, and trotted away.

II

A fox had used all his blandishments in vain, for he could not flatter the crow in the tree and make him drop the cheese he held in his beak. Suddenly, the crow tossed the cheese to the astonished fox. Just then the farmer, from whose kitchen the loot had been stolen, appeared, carrying a rifle, looking for the robber. The fox turned and ran for the woods. "There goes the guilty son of a vixen now!" cried the crow, who, in case you do not happen to know it, can see the glint of sunlight on a gun barrel at a greater distance than anybody.

III

This time the fox, who was determined not to be outfoxed by a crow, stood his ground and did not run when the farmer appeared, carrying a rifle and looking for the robber.

"The teeth marks in this cheese are mine," said the fox, "but the beak marks were made by the true culprit up there in the tree. I submit this cheese in evidence, as Exhibit A, and bid you and the criminal a very good day." Whereupon he lit a cigarette and strolled away.

IV

In the great and ancient tradition, the crow in the tree with the cheese in his beak began singing, and the cheese fell into the fox's lap. "You sing like a shovel," said the fox, with a grin, but the crow pretended not to hear and cried out, "Quick, give me back the cheese! Here comes the farmer with his rifle!"

"Why should I give you back the cheese?" the wily fox demanded.

"Because the farmer has a gun, and I can fly faster than you can run."

So the frightened fox tossed the cheese back to the crow, who ate it, and said, "Dearie me, my eyes are playing tricks on me—or am I playing tricks on you? Which do you think?" But there was no reply, for the fox had slunk away into the woods.

The Bears
and the Monkeys

IN A DEEP FOREST there lived many bears.
They spent the winter sleeping, and the
summer playing leap-bear and stealing honey
and buns from nearby cottages. One day a fast-
talking monkey named Glib showed up and
told them that their way of life was bad for

bears. "You are prisoners of pastime," he said, "addicted to leap-bear, and slaves of honey and buns."

The bears were impressed and frightened as Glib went on talking. "Your forebears have done this to you," he said. Glib was so glib, glibber than the glibbest monkey they had ever seen before, that the bears believed he must know more than they knew, or than anybody else. But when he left, to tell other species what was the matter with *them*, the bears reverted to their fun and games and their theft of buns and honey.

Their decadence made them bright of eye, light of heart, and quick of paw, and they had a wonderful time, living as bears had always lived, until one day two of Glib's successors appeared, named Monkey Say and Monkey Do. They were even glibber than Glib, and they brought many presents and smiled all the time. "We have come to liberate you from freedom," they said. "This is the New Liberation, twice as good as the old, since there are two of us."

So each bear was made to wear a collar, and the collars were linked together with chains, and Monkey Do put a ring in the lead bear's nose, and a chain on the lead bear's ring. "Now you are free to do what I tell you to do," said Monkey Do.

"Now you are free to say what I want you to say," said Monkey Say. "By sparing you the burden of electing your leaders, we save you from the dangers of choice. No more secret ballots, everything open and aboveboard."

For a long time the bears submitted to the New Liberation, and chanted the slogan the monkeys had taught them: "Why stand on your own two feet when you can stand on ours?"

Then one day they broke the chains of their new freedom and found their way back to the deep forest and began playing leap-bear again and stealing honey and buns from the nearby cottages. And their laughter and gaiety rang through the forest, and birds that had ceased singing began singing again, and all the sounds of the earth were like music.

MORAL: *It is better to have the ring of freedom in your ears than in your nose.*

50

The Father
and His Daughter

A LITTLE GIRL was given so many picture books on her seventh birthday that her father, who should have run his office and let her mother run the home, thought his daughter should give one or two of her new books to a little neighbor boy named Robert, who had dropped in, more by design than by chance.

Now, taking books, or anything else, from a little girl is like taking arms from an Arab, or candy from a baby, but the father of the little girl had his way and Robert got two of her books. "After all, that leaves you with nine," said the father, who thought he was a philosopher and a child psychologist, and couldn't shut his big fatuous mouth on the subject.

A few weeks later, the father went to his library to look up "father" in the Oxford English Dictionary, to feast his eyes on the praise of fatherhood through the centuries, but he couldn't find volume F-G, and then he discovered that three others were missing, too—A-B, L-M, and V-Z. He began a probe of his household, and soon learned what had become of the four missing volumes.

"A man came to the door this morning," said his little daughter, "and he didn't know how to get from here to Torrington, or from Torrington to Winsted, and he was a nice man, much nicer than Robert, and so I gave him four of your books. After all, there are thirteen volumes in the Oxford English Dictionary, and that leaves you nine."

MORAL: *This truth has been known from here to Menander: what's sauce for the gosling's not sauce for the gander.*

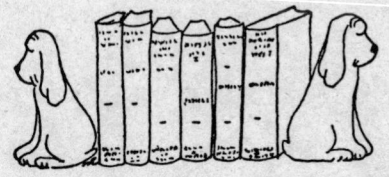

The Cat in the Lifeboat

A FELINE NAMED WILLIAM got a job as copy cat on a daily paper and was surprised to learn that every other cat on the paper was named Tom, Dick, or Harry. He soon found out that he was the only cat named William in town. The fact of his singularity went to his head, and he began confusing it with distinction. It got so that whenever he saw or heard the name William, he thought it referred to him. His fantasies grew wilder and wilder, and he came to believe that he was the Will of Last Will and Testament, and the Willy of Willy Nilly, and the cat who put the cat in catnip. He finally became convinced that Cadillacs were Catillacs because of him.

William became so lost in his daydreams that he no longer heard the editor of the paper when he shouted, "Copy cat!" and he became not only a ne'er-do-well, but a ne'er-do-anything. "You're fired," the editor told him one morning when he showed up for dreams.

"God will provide," said William jauntily.

"God has his eye on the sparrow," said the editor.

"So've I," said William smugly.

William went to live with a cat-crazy woman

who had nineteen other cats, but they could not stand William's egotism or the tall tales of his mythical exploits, honors, blue ribbons, silver cups, and medals, and so they all left the woman's house and went to live happily in huts and hovels. The cat-crazy woman changed her will and made William her sole heir, which seemed only natural to him, since he believed that all wills were drawn in his favor. "I am eight feet tall," William told her one day, and she smiled and said, "I should say you are, and I am going to take you on a trip around the world and show you off to everybody."

William and his mistress sailed one bitter March day on the S.S. *Forlorna,* which ran into heavy weather, high seas, and hurricane. At midnight the cargo shifted in the towering seas, the ship listed menacingly, SOS calls were frantically sent out, rockets were fired into the sky, and the officers began running up and down companionways and corridors shouting, "Abandon ship!" And then another shout arose, which seemed only natural to the egotistical cat. It was, his vain ears told him, the loud repetition of "William and children first!" Since William figured no lifeboat would be launched until he was safe and sound, he dressed leisurely, putting on white tie and tails, and then sauntered out on deck. He leaped lightly into a lifeboat that was being lowered, and found himself in the company of a little boy named Johnny Green and another little boy named Tommy Trout, and their mothers, and other children and their mothers. "Toss that cat overboard!" cried the sailor in charge of the lifeboat, and Johnny Green threw him overboard, but Tommy Trout pulled him back in.

"Let *me* have that tomcat," said the sailor, and he took William in his big right hand and threw him, like a long incompleted forward pass, about forty yards from the tossing lifeboat.

When William came to in the icy water, he

had gone down for the twenty-fourth time, and had thus lost eight of his lives, so he only had one left. With his remaining life and strength he swam and swam until at last he reached the sullen shore of a sombre island inhabited by surly tigers, lions, and other great cats. As William lay drenched and panting on the shore, a jaguar and a lynx walked up to him and asked him who he was and where he came from. Alas, William's dreadful experience in the lifeboat and the sea had produced traumatic amnesia, and he could not remember who he was or where he came from.

"We'll call him Nobody," said the jaguar.

"Nobody from Nowhere," said the lynx.

And so William lived among the great cats on the island until he lost his ninth life in a barroom brawl with a young panther who had asked him what his name was and where he came from and got what he considered an uncivil answer.

The great cats buried William in an unmarked grave because, as the jaguar said, "What's the good of putting up a stone reading 'Here lies Nobody from Nowhere'?"

MORAL: *O why should the spirit of mortal be proud, in this little voyage from swaddle to shroud?*

The Bragdowdy

A FEMALE HARE, who had been born with a foot in everybody's affairs, became known in her community as "that big Belgian busybody." She was always listening to the thumpings of her neighbors. "You're all ears," her mate snarled one day. "For God's sake, get some *laissez faire*." There was no answer, for she had hopped next door to exhort, reproach, and upbraid a female guinea pig who had borne one hundred and seventy-three young and had then let herself go. She had become a bragdowdy, and spent her time weeping over *True Pigtales*.

"Where is your civic spirit?" demanded Mrs. Hare. "And your country, state, federal,

and the Busybody

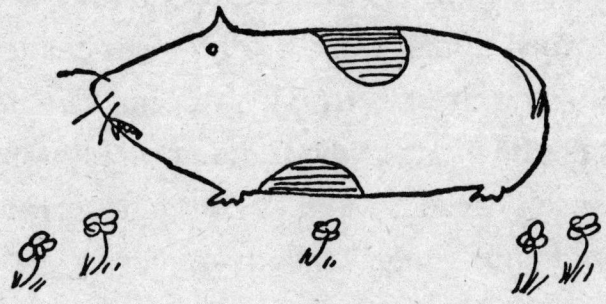

and global spirit? Look at me. I am president, or chairwoman, of practically everything, and founder of the Listening Post, an organization of eight hundred females with their ears to the ground."

The male guinea pig, who had been lying on a lettuce leaf, taking it easy, tried to hide from his nosy neighbor, but she came into the room, buttocky buttocky, before he could get out of bed.

"A big strapping male like you," she scoffed, "lying around the house when you ought to be at the laboratory, having injections to see whether some new serum is deadly or not." The male guinea pig's teeth began to chatter, and when a male guinea pig's teeth chatter it doesn't mean he's afraid, it means he's mad. But the Belgian busybody didn't care how anybody felt except herself. "You and your mate should join things and do things!" she exclaimed. "Shoulder to the wheel, nose to the grindstone, best foot forward, finger in the pie, knee on the chest!"

Before many weeks had passed, Mrs. Pig developed a guilt complex that manifested itself in an activity compulsion. She gave up reading *True Pigtales*, took her mate's edible bed away from him, straightened up the house, and joined twenty-four up-and-coming organizations. She became famous for keeping everybody on his toes, whether that's where he wanted to be or not. She was made chairman of the Bear a Basket of Babies Committee, secretary of the Get Behind Your Mate and Push Movement, treasurer of the Don't Let Dad Dawdle League, inventor of its slogan, "He can do twice as much in half the time if he puts your mind to it," and, in the end, national president of the Daughters of Ambitious Rodents.

The now celebrated Mrs. Pig also found time to bear thirty-seven more offspring, which was thirty-seven more than her mate had wanted. They drove him to Distraction, where he found the male Belgian hare, who had been driven there by his own mate's private and public projects, pryings, proddings, and pushings. The two males had such a quiet and peaceful time together without their mates that they decided to keep it that way. Representatives of ninety-six different organizations—

the seventy-two Mrs. Hare belonged to and Mrs. Pig's twenty-four—argued with them in vain. They ran away one night while their mates were addressing the He Could If He Wanted To, He's Just Not Trying Club, without so much as a fare-thee-well or a note on a pillow, and leaving no forwarding address. They decided to go to Tahiti to forget, but long before they reached Tahiti they had forgot.

MORAL: *Thou shalt not convert thy neighbor's wife, nor yet louse up thy neighbor's life.*

The Human Being
and the Dinosaur

AGES AGO in a wasteland of time and a wilderness of space, Man, in upper case, and dinosaur, in lower, first came face to face. They stood like stones for a long while, wary and watchful, taking each other in. Something told the dinosaur that he beheld before him the coming glory and terror of the world, and in the still air of the young planet he seemed to catch the faint smell of his own inevitable doom.

"Greetings, stupid," said Man. "Behold in me the artfully articulated architect of the future, the chosen species, the certain survivor, the indestructible one, the monarch of all you survey, and of all that everyone else surveys, for that matter. On the other hand, you are, curiously enough, for all your size, a member of the inconsequent ephemera. You are one of God's moderately amusing early experiments, a frail footnote to natural history, a contraption in a museum for future Man to marvel at, an excellent example of Jehovah's jejune juvenilia."

The dinosaur sighed with a sound like thunder.

"Perpetuating your species," Man continued, "would be foolish and futile."

"The missing link is not lost," said the dinosaur sorrowfully. "It's hiding."

Man paid the doomed dinosaur no mind. "If there were no Man it would be necessary to create one," said Man, "for God moves in mysterious, but inefficient, ways, and He needs help. Man will go on forever, but you will be one with the mammoth and the mastodon, for

monstrosity is the behemother of extinction."

"There are worse things than being extinct," said the dinosaur sourly, "and one of them is being you."

Man strutted a little pace and flexed his muscles. "You cannot even commit murder," he said, "for murder requires a mind. You are capable only of dinosaurslaughter. You and your ilk are incapable of devising increasingly effective methods of destroying your own species and, at the same time, increasingly miraculous methods of keeping it extant. You will never live to know the two-party system, the multi-party system, and the one-party system. You will be gone long before I have made this the best of all possible worlds, no matter how possible all other worlds may be. In your highest state of evolution you could not develop the brain cells to prove innocent men guilty, even after their acquittal. You are all wrong in the crotch, and in the cranium, and in the cortex. But I have wasted enough time on you. I must use these fingers which God gave me, and now probably wishes He had kept for Himself, to begin writing those noble volumes about Me which will one day run to several hundred billion items, many of them about war, death, conquest, decline, fall, blood, sweat, tears, threats, warnings, boasts, hopelessness, hell, heels, and whores. There will be little enough about you and your ilk and your kith and your kin, for after all, who were you and your ilk and your kith and your kin? Good day and goodbye," said Man in conclusion. "I shall see to it that your species receives a decent burial, with some simple ceremony."

Man, as it turned out, was right. The dinosaur and his ilk and his kith and his kin died not long after, still in lower case, but with a curious smile of satisfaction, or something of the sort, on their ephemeral faces.

MORAL: *The noblest study of mankind is Man, says Man.*

The Hen Party

ALL THE HENS came to Lady Buff Orpington's tea party and, as usual, Minnie
Minorca was the last to arrive, for, as usual, she
had spent the day with her psychiatrist, her
internist, and her beak, comb, and gizzard spe-

cialist. "I'm not long for this barnyard," she told the other hens. "What do you suppose I've got *now*?" She went about the room, giving all the hens a peck except her hostess, who pecked her, but without affection.

"I've got blue comb," Minnie went on.

A chill had fallen upon the gathering, as it always did when Minnie Minorca began reciting her complaints, old and new, real and hysterical. "Dr. Leghorn found out today that I am edentulous, and he told me so," said Minnie, triumphantly. "Of course I've always had chronic coryza, Newcastle disease, and laryngotracheitis."

"Minnie has so many pains she has given each of us one," said Lady Buff Orpington coldly. "Isn't that nice?"

"I love you girls," said Minnie, "and I love to share my troubles with you. You're such good listeners. I was telling my psychiatrist about my new ailments, including incipient dry feather, and he suddenly blurted out some of the things he has been keeping from me all these years. He said I have galloping aggression, inflamed ego, and too much gall."

"Now there's a psychiatrist who knows what he's talking about," said Miss Brahma, and she tried to talk to her hostess about the weather, and the other hens tried to talk to one another, but Minnie Minorca kept on telling how charged with punishments her scroll was. As she rambled on, describing in detail the attack of scale foot she had had in Cadawcutt, Connecticut, one of the hens whispered, "I've just put some sleeping pills in her teacup."

"You must have some more tea," cried Lady Buff Orpington, as she refilled Minnie's cup, and all her guests repeated, "You must have some more tea," and Minnie Minorca, delighted to be the center of attention and, as she thought, concern, hastily drank the slugged tea. After she had passed out, one of the hens suggested that they wring her neck while the wringing was good. "We could say she broke her neck trying to see what was the matter with her tail," the conspirator suggested.

Lady Buff Orpington sighed and said, "We'll draw lots to see who wrings her neck at the next tea party someone gives. Now let's go out and take a dust bath and leave old Fuss and Fevers to her nightmares." And the hostess and her guests went out into the road, leaving Minnie Minorca to dream of a brand new ailment, called Minnieitis, or Mrs. Minorca's disease.

MORAL: *Misery's love of company oft goeth unrequited.*

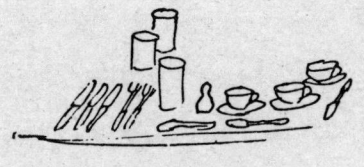

The Rose, the Fountain, and the Dove

IN A GREEN VALLEY, serene as a star and silent as the moon—except for the Saturday laughter of children and the sound of summer thunder—a rose and a fountain grew restless as time crept on.

"This is our sorrow: We're here today and here tomorrow," sighed the rose. "I wish I were rootloose and fancy-free, like the dove."

"I want to see what's in the wood," the fountain said. "I want to have adventures to cherish and regret." He signalled the dove in a cipher of sparkle, and the dove came down from the sky and made a graceful landing.

"What's in the wood?" the fountain asked. "You have wings and you must know, for there's nowhere you cannot go."

"I like to fly above the green valley," said the dove. "The green valley is all I know, and all I want to know."

"Stars fall in a pool in the wood," the rose declared. "I hear them sputter when they strike the water. I could fish them up and dry them out and sell them to a king, if I had wings like you," she told the dove.

"I like it where I am," the dove replied, "flying above the valley. I watch the stars that do not fall, and would not want to sell them."

"It is always the same wherever one is," complained the rose.

"To my eye, it is always changing," said the dove.

"I am weary of playing in this one spot forever," whimpered the fountain. "The same old patterns every day. Help, help, another spray!"

"There's nothing in the wood, I think, but horned owls in hollow oaks," the dove declared, "and violets by mossy stones."

"Violence by mossy stones is what I crave!" the fountain cried. "I'd love to meet the waterfall in silver combat, and damned be him who first dries up!"

"I have nothing to remember and nothing to forget," sighed the rose. "I waste my sweetness on the verdant air."

"I like it here" was all the dove would say. But the rose and the fountain kept after him every day of every week, and when the summer waned, they convinced the dove he loved the wood, admired horned owls, and ought to spend his life salvaging stars and meeting waterfalls in silver combat.

So the dove flew away into the wood and never came back. There were many varied rumors of the nature of his end. The four winds whispered that the dove had ceased to be because of mossy stones, half-hidden violets, or violence, malicious waterfalls, and owls in trees, but the wood thrush contended the dove had died while playing with burning stars. One thing was sure: The dove had ended the way no other dove had ever ended.

MORAL: *He who lives another's life another's death must die.*

The Bachelor Penguin
and the Virtuous Mate

ONE SPRING a bachelor penguin's fancy lightly turned, as it did in every season, to thoughts of illicit love. It was this gay seducer's custom to make passes at the more desirable females after their mates had gone down to the sea to fish. He had found out that all the females in the community made a ritual of rearranging the sitting-room furniture, putting it back where it had been the day before, and they were only too glad to have a strong male help them move the heavier pieces. Their mates had grown less and less interested in housework and more and more addicted to fishing, as time went on. The bachelor penguin proved handy at putting on or taking off screen doors, removing keys wedged in locks meant for other keys, and rescuing the females from

other quandaries of their own making. After a few visits, the feathered Don Juan induced the ladies to play Hide-in-the-Dark with him, and Guess Who This Is?, and Webfooty-Webfooty.

As the seasons rolled on, the handsome and well-groomed Casanova became a little jaded by his routine successes with the opposite sex. Then one morning, after the other male penguins had gone to the seashore to fish as usual, Don J. Penguin spied the prettiest female he had ever seen, trying, all by herself,

to move a sitting-room sofa back to the spot where it had been the day before. Don gallantly offered to help the matron in distress and she gladly accepted, with a shy look and a faint blush. The next morning the bachelor, who knew how to play his cards, came back and helped the housepenguin put on the screen door, and the following day he fixed the broken catch of her necklace, and the day after that he tightened the glass top of her percolator. Each time that he suggested playing Hide-in-the-Dark or Guess Who This Is?, the object of his desire thought of something else for him to fix, or loosen, or tighten, or take off, or put on. After several weeks of this, the amorist began to suspect that he was being taken, and his intended victim corroborated his fears.

"Unless you keep on helping me take things off, and put things on, and pry things loose, and make things tighter," she told the dismayed collector of broken hearts, "I will tell my mate about your improper advances and your dishonorable intentions." Don Penguin knew that the clever penguin's mate was the strongest male in the community, and also had the shortest temper and the least patience. There wasn't going to be any Hide-in-the-Dark or Guess Who This Is? or Webfooty-Webfooty. And so he spent the rest of his days working for the virtuous and guileful lady of his desire, moving sofas, taking things off and putting things on, loosening this and tightening that, and performing whatever other tasks his fair captor demanded of him. His bow tie became untied, his dinner jacket lost its buttons, his trousers lost their crease, and his eyes lost their dream. He babbled of clocks, and of keys caught in locks, and everybody closed her door when he came waddling down the street except the penguin who had taken him in with a beauty as unattainable as the stars, and a shy look, and a faint blush as phony as a parrot's laugh. One day her mate, returning early from the sea, caught a glimpse of Don leaving the house, and said, "What did old Droop Feather want?"

"Oh, he washes the windows and waxes the floors and sweeps the chimney," the female replied. "I believe he had an unhappy love affair."

MORAL: *One man's mate may sometimes be another man's prison.*

The Peacelike Mongoose

IN COBRA COUNTRY a mongoose was born one day who didn't want to fight cobras or anything else. The word spread from mongoose to mongoose that there was a mongoose who didn't want to fight cobras. If he didn't want to fight anything else, it was his own business, but it was the duty of every mongoose to kill cobras or be killed by cobras.

"Why?" asked the peacelike mongoose, and

the word went around that the strange new mongoose was not only pro-cobra and anti-mongoose but intellectually curious and against the ideals and traditions of mongoosism.

"He is crazy," cried the young mongoose's father.

"He is sick," said his mother.

"He is a coward," shouted his brothers.

"He is a mongoosexual," whispered his sisters.

Strangers who had never laid eyes on the peacelike mongoose remembered that they had seen him crawling on his stomach, or trying on cobra hoods, or plotting the violent overthrow of Mongoosia.

"I am trying to use reason and intelligence," said the strange new mongoose.

"Reason is six-sevenths of treason," said one of his neighbors.

"Intelligence is what the enemy uses," said another.

Finally, the rumor spread that the mongoose had venom in his sting, like a cobra, and he was tried, convicted by a show of paws, and condemned to banishment.

MORAL: *Ashes to ashes, and clay to clay, if the enemy doesn't get you your own folks may.*

The Godfather
and His Godchild

A WORLDLY-WISE COLLECTOR, who had trotted the globe collecting everything he could shoot, or buy, or make off with, called upon his godchild, a little girl of five, after a year of collecting in various countries of the world.

"I want to give you three things," he said. "Any three things your heart desires. I have diamonds from Africa, and a rhinoceros horn, scarabs from Egypt, emeralds from Guatemala, chessmen of ivory and gold, mooses' antlers, signal drums, ceremonial gongs, temple bells, and three rare and remarkable dolls. Now tell me," he concluded, patting the little girl on the head, "what do you want more than anything else in the world?"

His little godchild, who was not a hesitater, did not hesitate. "I want to break your glasses and spit on your shoes," she said.

MORAL: *Though statisticians in our time have never kept the score, Man wants a great deal here below and Woman even more.*

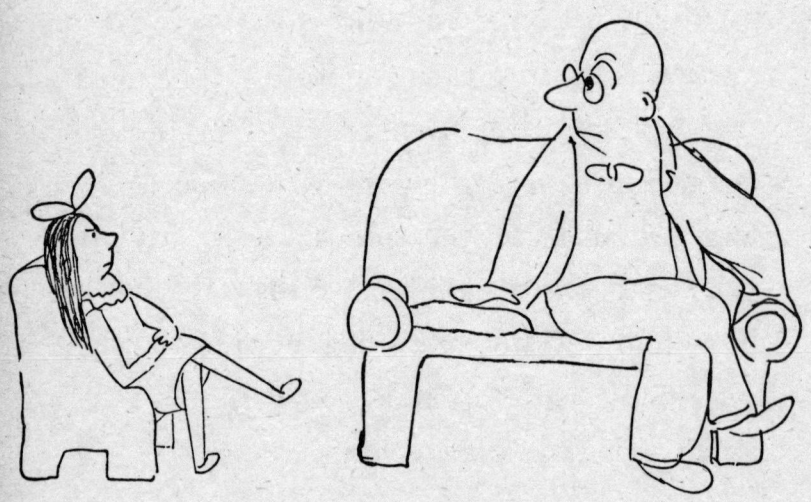

The Grizzly
and the Gadgets

A GRIZZLY BEAR who had been on a bender for several weeks following a Christmas party in his home at which his brother-in-law had set the Christmas tree on fire, his children had driven the family car through the front door and out the back, and all the attractive female bears had gone into hibernation before sunset returned home prepared to forgive, and live and let live. He found, to his mild annoyance, that the doorbell had been replaced by an ornamental knocker. When he lifted the knocker, he was startled to hear it play two bars of "Silent Night."

When nobody answered his knock, he turned the doorknob, which said "Happy New Year" in a metallic voice, and a two-tone gong rang "Hello" somewhere deep within the house.

He called to his mate, who was always the first to lay the old aside, as well as the first by whom the new was tried, and got no answer. This was because the walls of his house had been soundproofed by a soundproofer who had soundproofed them so well nobody could hear anybody say anything six feet away. Inside the living room the grizzly bear turned

on the light switch, and the lights went on all right, but the turning of the switch had also released an odor of pine cones, which this particular bear had always found offensive. The head of the house, now becoming almost as angry as he had been on Christmas Day, sank into an easy chair and began bouncing up and down and up and down, for it was a brand-new contraption called "Sitpretty" which made you bounce up and down and up and down when you sat on it. Now thoroughly exasperated, the bear jumped up from the chair and began searching for a cigarette. He found a cigarette box, a new-fangled cigarette box he had never seen before, which was made of metal and plastic in the shape of a castle, complete with portal and drawbridge and tower. The trouble was that the bear couldn't get the thing open. Then he made out, in tiny raised letters on the portal, a legend in rhyme: "You can have a cigarette on me If you can find the castle key." The bear could not find the castle

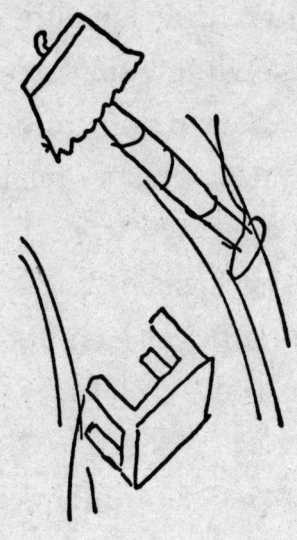

the mantelpiece, and overturned chairs and tables, growling and howling and roaring, shouting and bawling and cursing, until his wife was aroused from a deep dream of marrying a panda, neighbors appeared from blocks around, and the attractive female bears who had gone into hibernation began coming out of it to see what was going on.

The bear, deaf to the pleas of his mate, heedless of his neighbors' advice, and unafraid of the police, kicked over whatever was still standing in the house, and went roaring away for good, taking the most attractive of the attractive female bears, one named Honey, with him.

MORAL: *Nowadays most men lead lives of noisy desperation.*

The Goose That Laid
the Gilded Egg

THE GOOSE didn't really lay a gilded egg.
She laid an ordinary goose egg, like any
other goose egg, and some joker gilded it when
she left the nest for a snack or a snail. When
she came back and saw the gleaming surprise,

she cried, "Lo, I have laid the golden egg of lore and legend!"

"Lo, my foot," said a Plymouth Rock hen. "That is an ordinary goose egg painted yellow, if you ask me."

"She isn't asking you," said a rooster. "She is asking me, and I say that is a solid-gold egg."

The goose did not seem overjoyed. "I had my heart set on raising a gosling," she said.

"You'll have a golden gosling," said the rooster.

"Golden gosling, my feathers," said the hen. "She'll have a yellow gosling, like any other yellow gosling, only punier."

"I don't care what it looks like," said the goose. "I just don't want it to be gold. People would talk. They would snatch my quills for souvenirs. I would be photographed all the time."

"I will offer you a fabulous sum for that glittering miracle," said the rooster, and he named a sum fabulous only as things are figured fiscally among the feathered. The goose gladly accepted the offer.

"I wouldn't sit on that egg," said the hen. "I wouldn't sit on it if a platinum gander encrusted with diamonds came out of it."

"I'll sit on it myself," said the rooster.

And so the hopeful rooster rolled the gilded goose egg to a nest and began sitting on it. At the end of three weeks, all the hens left his bed and board.

"You'll be sorry," said the rooster, "when this priceless treasure is hatched. I know it will be a golden goose. I have already named her— Goldie. When she becomes a full-grown goose, I will sell her to the highest bidder for a superfabulous sum."

"Oh, sure," said the Plymouth Rock hen, "and my family came over on the Mayflower," and she went away.

The old positivist sat and sat and sat on the gilded egg, and all his friends drifted away, and no hen would look at him, and his feathers began to fall out. One day, being a male and not a female, he clumsily stepped on the egg and broke it, and that was the end of the egg and the end of his dreams.

MORAL: *It is wiser to be hendubious than cocksure.*

The Trial of the
Old Watchdog

AN OLD experienced collie, who had been a faithful country watchdog for many years, was arrested one summer's day and accused of the first-degree murder of a lamb. Actually, the lamb had been slain by a notorious red fox who had planted the still-warm body of his victim in the collie's kennel.

The trial was held in a kangaroo court presided over by Judge Wallaby. The jury consisted of foxes, and all the spectators were foxes. A fox named Reynard was prosecuting attorney. "Morning, Judge," he said.

"God bless you, boy, and good luck," replied Judge Wallaby jovially.

A poodle named Beau, an old friend and neighbor of the collie, represented the accused watchdog. "Good morning, Judge," said the poodle.

"Now I don't want you to be too clever," the Judge warned him. "Cleverness should be confined to the weaker side. That's only fair."

A blind woodchuck was the first creature to take the stand, and she testified that she saw the collie kill the lamb.

"The witness is blind!" protested the poodle.

"No personalities, please," said the Judge severely. "Perhaps the witness saw the murder in a dream or a vision. This would give her testimony the authority of revelation."

"I wish to call a character witness," said the poodle.

"We have no character witnesses," said Reynard smoothly, "but we have some charming character assassins."

One of these, a fox named Burrows, was called to the stand. "I didn't actually see this lamb killer kill this lamb," said Burrows, "but I almost did."

"That's close enough," said Judge Wallaby.

"Objection," barked the poodle.

"Objection overruled," said the Judge. "It's getting late. Has the jury reached a verdict?"

The forefox of the jury stood up. "We find the defendant guilty," he said, "but we think it would be better to acquit him, nonetheless. If we hang the defendant, his punishment will be over. But if we acquit him of such dark crimes as murder, concealing the body, and associating with poodles and defense attorneys, nobody will ever trust him again, and he will be suspect all the days of his life. Hanging is too good for him, and much too quick."

"Guilt by exoneration!" Reynard cried. "What a lovely way to end his usefulness!"

And so the case was dismissed and court was adjourned, and everybody went home to tell about it.

MORAL: *Thou shalt not blindfold justice by pulling the wool over her eyes.*

The Philosopher
and the Oyster

B Y THE SEA on a lovely morning strolled a philosopher—one who seeks a magnificent explanation for his insignificance—and there he came upon an oyster lying in its shell upon the sand.

"It has no mind to be burdened by doubt," mused the philosopher, "no fingers to work to the bone. It can never say, 'My feet are killing me.' It hears no evil, sees no television, speaks no folly. It has no buttons to come off, no zipper to get caught, no hair or teeth to fall out." The philosopher sighed a deep sigh of envy. "It produces a highly lustrous concretion, of great price or priceless," he said, "when a morbid condition obtains in its anatomy, if you could call such an antic, anomalous amorphousness anatomy." The philosopher sighed again and said, "Would that I could wake from delirium with a circlet of diamonds upon my fevered brow. Would, moreover, that my house were my sanctuary, as sound and secure as a safe-deposit vault."

Just then a screaming sea gull swooped out of the sky, picked up the oyster in its claws, carried it high in the air, and let it drop upon a great wet rock, shattering the shell and splattering its occupant. There was no lustrous concretion, of any price whatever, among the de-

bris, for the late oyster had been a very healthy oyster, and, anyway, no oyster ever profited from its pearl.

MORALS: *Count your own blessings, and let your neighbor count his.*

Where there is no television, the people also perish.

Tea for One

A YOUNG HUSBAND was wakened at five o'clock one morning by his bride. "Is the house on fire?" he mumbled. She laughed merrily. "The dawn is here," she said, "and I am going to bake a sugar cake."

"I don't want a sugar cake, I want toast and coffee," the bridegroom said.

"The sugar cake's for you to take for all the boys to see," she explained.

"All what boys?" demanded her husband, who was still drowsy.

"The boys at the office, silly," she said. "Let them see it, and then bring it home, and maybe we'll have it for dinner."

He got up and started to dress.

"I'll make tea for both of us now," she said, singing the line, and adding, "Coffee doesn't rhyme with anything. You can't have coffee."

He had tied his shoes and was tying his tie, when her voice brightened and she clapped her hands. "We'll raise a family," she said gaily. "You can have the boy, and I'll take the girl." And she scampered down the stairs to start to bake the sugar cake for him to take for all the boys to see. When she had gone, the bridegroom glanced at his watch. It was eleven minutes after five. He brushed his teeth and combed his hair, and then he climbed out the bedroom window, dropped to the ground below, and slipped away into the dawn, to find an all-night restaurant where a man could get a meal a man could eat.

MORAL: *If life went along like a popular song, every man's marriage would surely go wrong.*

The Mouse
and the Money

A CITY MOUSE who moved to the country to live in the walls of an old house
with a lot of country mice began lording it over
them from the start. He trimmed his whiskers,
put *mousseline* in his hair, talked with an
accent, and told the country mice that they

came from the wrong side of the mouse tracks.

"My ancestors were of the French aristocracy," boasted the city mouse. "Our name still appears on bottles of great French wine: '*Mise du château*,' which means mice in the château, or castle mice." Every day the newcomer bragged about his forebears, and when he ran out of ancestors he made some up. "My great-great-great-grandfather was a theater mouse at the Comédie-Française, and he married a cathedral mouse, one of the cathedral mice of Chartres. At their wedding a dessert named in their honor, *mousse chocolat,* was served to millions of guests."

Then the city mouse told how his family had come to America in the bridal suite of a great French liner. "My brother is a restaurant mouse at '21,' and my sister's at the Metropolitan," he said. He went on to tell of other ancestors of the family who had been in such productions as *The Chauve Souris* and *Die Fledermaus* and *Les Trois Mousquetaires*. "Not a mouse in our house was a common house mouse," he said.

One day, wandering through forbidden walls of the country house, to show his inferiors that he knew his way around, he came upon a treasure in currency which someone had hidden years before between the plaster and the lath. "I wouldn't eat that stuff," warned an old country mouse. "It is the root of evil and it will give you greenback bellyache." But the city mouse did not listen.

"I'm already a mouse of distinction," said the city mouse, "and this money will make me a millionaire. I'll be loaded." So he began to eat the currency, which consisted of bills of large denominations, and he drove off one or two of the young country mice who wanted to help him eat the treasure, saying, "Finders are not their brothers' keepers." The city mouse told his country cousins, "Blessed are the rich, for they can pay their way into the kingdom of Heaven," and he got off a lot of other witticisms, such as "Legal tender is the night" and "Money makes the nightmare go."

And so he went on living, as he put it, on the fat of the lath. "When I have eaten it all," he said, "I shall return to the city and live like a king. They say you can't take it with you, but I'm going to take it with *me*."

In a few days and nights the arrogant city mouse with the fancy and fanciful French forebears had eaten all the money, which amounted to an ambassador's annual salary. Then he tried to leave the walls of the old country house, but he was so loaded with money, and his head was so swelled, that he got caught between the plaster and the lath and could not get out, and his neighbors could not dislodge him, and so he died in the walls, and nobody but the country mice knew that he had been the richest mouse in the world.

MORAL: *This is the posture of fortune's slave: one foot in the gravy, one foot in the grave.*

The Wolf
at the Door

Mr. and Mrs. Sheep were sitting in their sitting room with their daughter, who was as pretty as she was edible, when there was a knock at the front door. "It's a gentleman caller," said the daughter.

"It's the Fuller Brush man," said her mother.

The cautious father got up and looked out the window. "It's the wolf," he said. "I can see his tail."

"Don't be silly," said the mother. "It's the Fuller Brush man, and that's his brush." And she went to the door and opened it, and the wolf came in and ran away with the daughter.

"You were right, after all," admitted the mother, sheepishly.

MORAL: Mother doesn't *always* know best. (The italics are father's and daughter's and mine.)

What Happened to Charles

A FARM HORSE named Charles was led to town one day by his owner, to be shod. He would have been shod and brought back home without incident if it hadn't been for Eva, a duck, who was always hanging about the kitchen door of the farmhouse, eavesdropping, and never got anything quite right. Her farm-mates said of her that she had two mouths but only one ear.

On the day that Charles was led away to the smithy, Eva went quacking about the farm, excitedly telling the other animals that Charles had been taken to town to be shot.

"They're executing an innocent horse!" cried Eva. "He's a hero! He's a martyr! He died to make us free!"

"He was the greatest horse in the world," sobbed a sentimental hen.

"He just seemed like old Charley to me," said a realistic cow. "Let's not get into a moony mood."

"He was wonderful!" cried a gullible goose.

"What did he ever do?" asked a goat.

Eva, who was as inventive as she was inaccurate, turned on her lively imagination. "It was butchers who led him off to be shot!" she shrieked. "They would have cut our throats while we slept if it hadn't been for Charles!"

"I didn't see any butchers, and I can see a burnt-out firefly on a moonless night," said a barn owl. "I didn't hear any butchers, and I can hear a mouse walk across moss."

"We must build a memorial to Charles the Great, who saved our lives," quacked Eva. And all the birds and beasts in the barnyard except the wise owl, the skeptical goat, and the realistic cow set about building a memorial.

Just then the farmer appeared in the lane, leading Charles, whose new shoes glinted in the sunlight.

It was lucky that Charles was not alone, for the memorial-builders might have set upon him with clubs and stones for replacing their hero with just plain old Charley. It was lucky, too, that they could not reach the barn owl, who quickly perched upon the weathervane of the barn, for none is so exasperating as he who is right. The sentimental hen and the gullible goose were the ones who finally called attention to the true culprit—Eva, the one-eared duck with two mouths. The others set upon her and tarred and unfeathered her, for none is more unpopular than the bearer of sad tidings that turn out to be false.

MORAL: *Get it right or let it alone. The conclusion you jump to may be your own.*

The Daws on the Dial

A YOUNG JACKDAW told his father that he was going to build his nest on the minute hand of the town clock. "That's the most unthinkable thing you ever thought of," said old John Daw. Young Jack was not deterred. "We'll build our nest when the minute hand is level," he said, "at a quarter of or a quarter after."

"Those who live in castles in the air have nowhere to go but down," the old Daw warned, but Jack and his mate built their nest on the clock at a quarter after eight the next morning. At twenty minutes after eight the nest slipped off the minute hand and fell into the street below. "We didn't start early enough," the young Daw told his father that evening. "Better never than late. We'll try again tomorrow at a quarter after six."

"If at first you don't succeed, fail, fail again," said the elder Daw. But he might as well have been talking to a gargoyle. Jack and his mate stole some of the elder Daw's silverware and built their nest again the following morning, and again it slipped off the minute hand and fell into the street below.

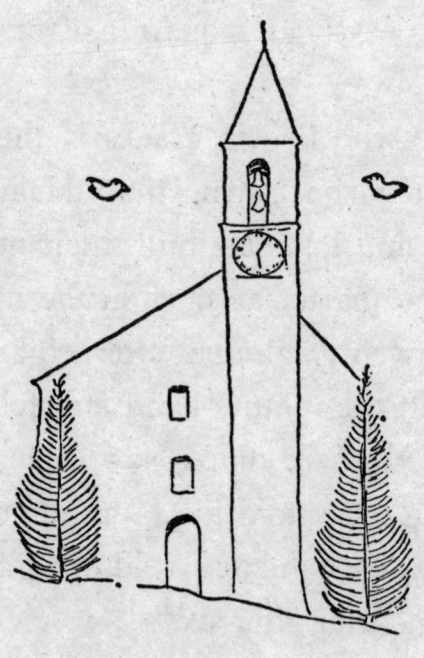

That evening old John Daw had more to say to his reckless offspring. "To stick on a dial, you would need three feet, one of them a rabbit's. Don't hang heavy on time's hands, just because it hangs heavy on yours. Clockwise is not wise enough. Even the cyclone and the merry-go-round know that much."

And again the young Daws did not listen, and again they swiped some silverware from his parents' nest to furnish their own. This time, those human beings known as municipal authorities were concealed in the clock tower, and, with brooms and yells and stones and bells, they frightened the foolish daws away from the clock and the tower and the town.

That night old John Daw's mate counted her silverware and sighed with dismay. "Gone, alas, with our youth, two spoons," she said, "and half the knives, and most of the forks, and all of the napkin rings."

"If I told him once, I told him a hundred times, 'Neither a burglar nor a lender be,'" raged old John, "but I might as well have been talking to a cast-iron lawn Daw." Not a word was heard from the young Daws as the weeks went on. "No news is bad news," grumbled old John Daw. "They have probably built their nest this time on a wagon wheel, or inside a bell."

He was wrong about that. The young Daws had built their last nest in the muzzle of a cannon, and they heard only the first gun of a twenty-one-gun salute fired in honor of a visiting chief of state.

MORAL: *The saddest words of pen or tongue are wisdom's wasted on the young.*

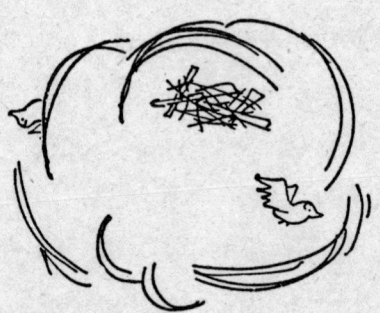

The Tiger Who Would Be King

ONE MORNING the tiger woke up in the jungle and told his mate that he was king of beasts.

"Leo, the lion, is king of beasts," she said.

"We need a change," said the tiger. "The creatures are crying for a change."

The tigress listened but she could hear no crying, except that of her cubs.

"I'll be king of beasts by the time the moon rises," said the tiger. "It will be a yellow moon with black stripes, in my honor."

"Oh, sure," said the tigress as she went to look after her young, one of whom, a male, very like his father, had got an imaginary thorn in his paw.

The tiger prowled through the jungle till he came to the lion's den. "Come out," he roared, "and greet the king of beasts! The king is dead, long live the king!"

Inside the den, the lioness woke her mate. "The king is here to see you," she said.

"What king?" he inquired, sleepily.

"The king of beasts," she said.

"I am the king of beasts," roared Leo, and he charged out of the den to defend his crown against the pretender.

It was a terrible fight, and it lasted until the setting of the sun. All the animals of the jungle joined in, some taking the side of the tiger and others the side of the lion. Every creature from the aardvark to the zebra took part in the struggle to overthrow the lion or to repulse the tiger, and some did not know which they were fighting for, and some fought for both, and some fought whoever was nearest, and some fought for the sake of fighting.

"What are we fighting for?" someone asked the aardvark.

"The old order," said the aardvark.

"What are we dying for?" someone asked the zebra.

"The new order," said the zebra.

When the moon rose, fevered and gibbous, it shone upon a jungle in which nothing stirred except a macaw and a cockatoo, screaming in horror. All the beasts were dead except the tiger, and his days were numbered and his time was ticking away. He was monarch of all he surveyed, but it didn't seem to mean anything.

MORAL: *You can't very well be king of beasts if there aren't any.*

The Chipmunk
and His Mate

A MALE CHIPMUNK could sleep like a top or a log or a baby as soon as his head hit the pillow, but his mate was always as wakeful as an owl or a nightwatchman or a burglar. When he turned the lights off, she would turn them on again and read, or worry, or write letters in her head, or wonder where things were. She was often drowsy after supper, and sometimes nodded in her chair, but she became

wide awake as soon as her head hit the pillow. She would lie there wondering if her mate had left his pistol in the nursery, what she had done with the Christmas tree ornaments, and whether or not she had left the fire on under the prunes. She was sure the wastebasket was smoldering in the living room, that she had left the kitchen door unlocked, and that someone was tiptoeing around downstairs.

The male chipmunk always slept until the sun was high, but his mate heard all the clocks strike all the hours. She could doze off in the daytime with a glass in her hand, or while her mate was reading aloud, or when his boss came to call, but as soon as she got in bed, she began writing letters in her head, or wondering if she had put the cat out, or where her handbag was, or why she hadn't heard from her mother.

One day she fell asleep while driving the family car, and, after a decent interval, the male chipmunk married her sister. He could still sleep like a top or a log or a baby, but his new mate just lay there as wide awake as an owl or a nightwatchman or a burglar, hearing intruders, smelling something burning, wondering if her mate had let his insurance lapse. One enchanted evening, across a crowded room, he met a stranger, an eight o'clock sleepy-time gal. They ran away to Maracaibo together, where they slept happily ever after. The second mate lay awake every night, wondering what the chipfrump had that she didn't have and what he saw in her, and whether she herself had put out the milk bottles or left the water running in the kitchen sink.

MORAL: *A man's bed is his cradle, but a woman's is often her rack.*

The Weaver
and the Worm

A WEAVER watched in wide-eyed wonder a silkworm spinning its cocoon in a white mulberry tree.

"Where do you get that stuff?" asked the admiring weaver.

"Do you want to make something out of it?" inquired the silkworm, eagerly.

Then the weaver and the silkworm went their separate ways, for each thought the other had insulted him. We live, man and worm, in a time when almost everything can mean almost anything, for this is the age of gobbledygook, doubletalk, and gudda.

MORAL: *A word to the wise is not sufficient if it doesn't make any sense.*

Two Dogs

ONE SULTRY moonless night, a leopard escaped from a circus and slunk away into the shadows of a city. The chief of police dogs assigned to the case a German shepherd named Plunger and a plainclothes bloodhound named Plod. Plod was a slow, methodical sleuth, but his uniformed partner was restless and impatient. Plod set the pace until Plunger snapped, "We couldn't catch a turtle this way," and bounded along the trail like a whippet. He got lost. When Plod found him, half an hour later, the bloodhound said, "It is better to get somewhere slowly than nowhere fast."

"Repose is for the buried," said the police dog. "I even chase cats in my dreams."

"I don't," said the bloodhound. "Out of scent, out of mind."

As they went along, each in his own way, through the moonlessness, they exchanged further observations on life.

"He who hunts and turns away may live to hunt another day," commented Plod.

"*Runs* away, you mean," sneered Plunger.

"I never run," said the bloodhound. "It's no good trailing a cat when you're out of breath, especially if the cat isn't. I figured that out myself. They call it instinct."

"I was taught to do what I do, and not to do what I don't," the police dog said. "They call it discipline. When *I* catch cats, cats stay caught," he added.

"I don't catch them, I merely find out where they are," the bloodhound said quietly.

The two dogs suddenly made out a great dark house looming in front of them at the end of a lane. "The trail ends right here, twenty feet from that window," the bloodhound said, sniffing a certain spot. "The leopard must have leaped into the house from here."

The two dogs stared into the open window of the dark and silent house.

"I was taught to jump through the open windows of dark houses," said Plunger.

"I taught myself not to," said Plod. "I wouldn't grab that cat if I were you. I never grab a leopard unless it is a coat." But Plunger wasn't listening.

"Here goes," he said jauntily, and he jumped through the window of the dark and silent house. Instantly there was a racket that sounded to the keen ears of the bloodhound like a police dog being forcibly dressed in women's clothes by a leopard, and that is precisely what it was. All of a moment, Plunger, dressed in women's clothes from hat to shoes, with a pink parasol thrust under his collar, came hurtling out the window. "I had my knee on his chest, too," said the bewildered police dog plaintively.

The old sleuth sighed. "He lasteth longest and liveth best who gets not his knee on his quarry's chest," murmured Plod, in cloudy English but fluent Bloodhound.

MORAL: *Who would avoid life's wriest laughter should not attain the thing he's after.*

The Lady of the Legs

IN A POOL NEAR PARIS there lived a frog who thought she was wonderful.

"I have the largest lily pad, the deepest dive, the prettiest eyes, and the finest voice in the world," she croaked.

"You also have the most succulent legs on earth or water," said a human voice one day. It was the voice of a renowned Parisian restaurateur, who was passing by when he heard all the bragging.

"I do not know what succulent means," said the frog.

"You must have the smallest vocabulary in the world," said the restaurateur, and the foolish frog, who took every superlative for praise, was pleased, and flushed a deeper green than ever.

"I should like to set you before a certain celebrated *bon vivant*," said the man, "a distinguished gourmet, a connoisseur of the *grande haute cuisine*."

The frog almost swooned with delight at the elegant sound of these strange words.

"You will be served like a queen," said the restaurateur. "Provençal. Under my personal supervision, of course."

"Tell me more," said the rapt and rapturous frog.

"You will be served with the most excellent vintage wine in the world," said the man. "A great Montrachet, I should think, would be perfect."

"Go on," urged the vain and foolish frog.

"You will be talked about whenever devotees of the culinary art assemble," said the restaurateur. "You will be remembered as the daintiest dish in the history of gastronomy."

At this the frog swooned in a transport of joy and an excess of misplaced self-esteem, and while she was unconscious, the renowned Parisian restaurateur deftly removed her succulent legs and took them to his restaurant, where they were prepared under his personal supervision as he had promised, and served, Provençal, with a bottle of Montrachet, to a celebrated *bon vivant*.

MORAL: *Fatua cruraque mox separabuntur.*

The Kingfisher
and the Phoebe

A PROUD MOTHER PHOEBE who had raised two broods of fledglings in the fair weather was at first dismayed and then delighted when one of the males of the second brood refused to leave the nest and fly away like the others. "I have raised a remarkable phoebe unlike any other phoebe," the mother bird decided. "He will become a great singer, greater than the nightingale."

She brought in a nightingale to teach her son to sing, and then a catbird, and then a mockingbird, but all the young phoebe could learn to sing was "Phoebe, Phoebe." And so the mother bird sent for Dr. Kingfisher, a bird psychologist, who examined the young phoebe carefully. "This phoebe is a phoebe like any other phoebe," he told the mother. "And all he will ever sing is 'Phoebe, Phoebe.'"

But the ambitious mother did not believe Dr. Kingfisher's prognosis. "Maybe he won't be a great singer, but he will be a great something," she insisted. "He will take the place of the eagle on the dollar, or the canary in the gilded cage, or the cuckoo in the cuckoo clock. You just wait."

"I'll wait," said Dr. Kingfisher, and he waited. But nothing happened. The phoebe went on being a phoebe and singing "Phoebe, Phoebe" like any other phoebe, and that was all.

MORAL: *You can't make anything out of cookie dough except cookies.*

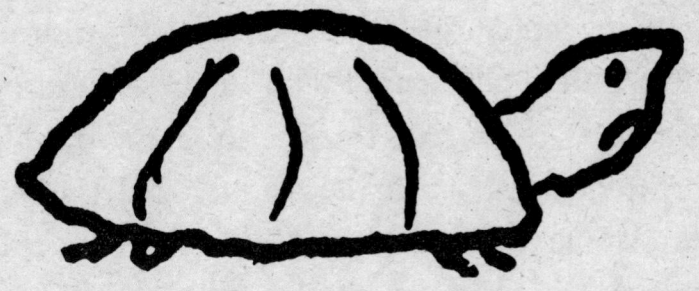

The Turtle Who
Conquered Time

A TURTLE appeared in a meadow one summer's day and attracted the attention of
all the creatures in the grass and in the trees,
because the date 44 B.C. was carved on his shell.
"Our meadow is honored indeed," exclaimed
a grasshopper, "for our visitor is the oldest of
all living creatures."

"We must build a pavilion in his honor," said a frog, and the catbirds and the swallows and the other birds built a stately pleasure dome out of twigs and leaves and blossoms for the very important turtle. An orchestra of crickets played music in his honor, and a wood thrush sang. The sounds of jubilee were heard in nearby fields and woods, and as more and more creatures turned up from farther and farther away to have a look at the ancient turtle, the grasshopper decided to charge admission to the pavilion.

"I will be the barker," said the frog, and, with the help of the grasshopper, he composed an impressive spiel. "Yesterday and yesterday and yesterday," it began, "creeps in this carapace from day to day to the first syllable of recorded time. This great turtle was born two thousand years ago, the year the mighty Julius Caesar died. Horace was twenty-one in 44 B.C., and Cicero had but a single year to live." The bystanders did not seem very much interested in the turtle's ancient contemporaries, but they gladly paid to go in and have a look at his ancient body.

Inside the pavilion, the grasshopper continued the lecture. "This remarkable turtle is a direct descendant of one of the first families of Ooze," he chanted. "His great-grandfather may have been the first thing that moved in the moist and muddy margins of this cooling planet. Except for our friend's ancestors, there was nothing but coal and blobs of glob."

One day a red squirrel who lived in a neighboring wood dropped in to look at the turtle and to listen to the ballyhoo. "Forty-four B.C., my foot!" scoffed the squirrel, as he glared at the grasshopper. "You are full of tobacco juice, and your friend the frog is full of lightning bugs. The carving of an ancient date on the carapace of a turtle is a common childish prank. This creep was probably born no earlier than 1902."

As the red squirrel ranted on, the spectators

who had paid to get into the pavilion began departing quietly, and there was no longer a crowd listening to the frog out front. The crickets put away their instruments and disappeared as silently as the Arabs, and the wood thrush gathered up his sheet music and flew off and did not return. The sounds of jubilee were no longer heard in the once merry meadow, and the summer seemed to languish like a dying swan.

"I knew all the time he wasn't two thousand years old," admitted the grasshopper, "but the legend pleased the people, young and old, and many smiled who had not smiled for years."

"And many laughed who had not laughed for years," said the frog, "and many eyes sparkled and many hearts were gay." The turtle shed a turtle tear at this and crawled away.

"The truth is not merry and bright," said the red squirrel. "The truth is cold and dark. Let's face it." And, looking smug and superior, the iconoclast scampered impudently back to his tree in the wood. From the grass of the meadow voices once carefree and gay joined in a rueful and lonely chorus, as if someone great and wonderful had died and was being buried.

MORAL: *Oh, why should the shattermyth have to be a crumplehope and a dampenglee?*

The Lion

A LION and a lizard kept the halls where once a prince had slept. The prince had died, as even princes do, and his palace had fallen to rats and ruin. The lion destroyed the rats, but he could never find the lizard, who lived in a crevice in the wall. There was royal food in the ruined kitchen, and royal wine in the ruined cellar, but the lion got it all, for the lizard was afraid to emerge from his hiding place. So the lion got fatter and fatter, and drunker and drunker, and the lizard grew thinner and thinner, and soberer and soberer. Weeks went by, and the weeds grew and the walls crumbled, as the lion ate six meals a day, washing them down with a total of eighteen different wines. One night, as the tawny master of the palace was topping off his sixth meal of the day with a tankard of brandy, he fell asleep on his golden chair at the head of the ornate

and the Lizard

table. The lizard, with his remaining strength, which wasn't much, crawled up on the table and tried to nibble a crumb, but he was too weak to eat. The lion, awakened by a tiny tinkle of spoons, tried to crush the unwelcome guest with one blow of his mighty paw, but he was sated and obese, and his paw was no longer mighty. He passed away in his golden chair, spilling the last of the brandy, as the lizard gave up the ghost among the crumbs and silver.

MORAL: *He who dies of a surfeit is as dead as he who starves.*

The Tigress
and Her Mate

P ROUDFOOT, a tiger, became tired of his
mate, Sabra, a few weeks after they had
set up housekeeping, and he fell to leaving
home earlier and earlier in the morning, and
returning later and later at night. He no

longer called her "Sugar Paw," or anything else, but merely clapped his paws when he wanted anything, or, if she was upstairs, whistled. The last long speech he ever made to her at breakfast was "What the hell's the matter with you? I bring you rice and peas and coconut oil, don't I? Love is something you put away in the attic with your wedding dress. Forget it." And he finished his coffee, put down the *Jungle News*, and started for the door.

"Where are you going?" Sabra asked.

"Out," he said. And after that, every time she asked him where he was going, he said, "Out," or "Away," or "Hush."

When Sabra became aware of the coming of what would have been, had she belonged to the chosen species, a blessed event, and told Proudfoot about it, he snarled, "Growp." He had now learned to talk to his mate in code, and "growp" meant "I hope the cubs grow up to be xylophone players or major generals." Then he went away, as all male tigers do at such a moment, for he did not want to be bothered by his young until the males were old enough to box with and the females old enough to insult. While waiting for the unblessed event to take place, he spent his time fighting water buffaloes and riding around with plain-clothes tigers in a prowl car.

When he finally came home, he said to his mate, "Eeps," meaning "I'm going to hit the sack, and if the kids keep me awake by yowling, I'll drown them like so many common house kittens." Sabra stalked to the front door of their house, opened it, and said to her mate, "Scat." The fight that took place was terrible but brief. Proudfoot led with the wrong paw, was nailed with the swiftest right cross in the jungle, and never really knew where he was after that. The next morning, when the cubs, male and female, tumbled eagerly down the stairs demanding to know what they could do, their mother said, "You can go in the parlor and play with your father. He's the tiger rug just in front of the fireplace. I hope you'll like him."

The children loved him.

MORAL: *Never be mean to a tiger's wife, especially if you're the tiger.*

The Magpie's Treasure

ONE DAY when the sun made everything that glitters glitter and everything that sparkles sparkle, a magpie picked up something from a gutter and carried it off to her nest. A crow and a rabbit had seen her swoop down and fly away, and each decided she had found something good to eat. "I'm sure it's a carrot," said the rabbit, "for I heard her say something about carrots."

"I saw it glitter," said the crow, "and it glittered edibly, like a yellow grain of corn."

"Corn is for the commoner," said the rabbit scornfully.

"You can have your carrots, and welcome to them," said the crow. They smacked their lips as they approached the magpie's nest. "I'll find out what she's got," said the crow. "If it's a grain of corn, I'll eat it. If it's a carrot, I'll throw it down to you."

So the crow flew to the edge of the magpie's nest while the rabbit waited below. The magpie happily showed the crow what she had found in the gutter. "It's a fourteen-carat diamond set in a golden ring," she said. "I wanted rings from the time I could fly, but my parents were worm collectors. If I had had my way, I'd be a wealthy bird today, surrounded by rings and other lovely things."

"You are living in the pluperfect subjunctive," said the crow disdainfully.

"It's serene there, and never crowded, except for old regrets," the magpie said.

The crow dropped down to the ground and explained to the rabbit that the "carrots" the magpie had talked about were only carats. "One carrot is worth fourteen carats," the rabbit said. "You can multiply that by twenty and it will still be true."

"If I can't eat it, I don't want it," said the crow. "Seeing is deceiving. It's eating that's believing." And the crow and the rabbit swallowed their disappointment, for want of anything else, and left the magpie to the enjoyment of her treasure. The light made everything that sparkles sparkle, and everything that glitters glitter, and the magpie was content until the setting of the sun.

MORAL: Chacun à son gout *is very very true, but why should we despise the apples of other eyes?*

The Cricket
and the Wren

AT A MUSIC FESTIVAL one summer in Tangletale Wood, a score of soloists came together to compete for the annual Peacock Awards. The Cricket was asked to pick the winner because of his fame as a fiddler and his many appearances on radio, where he is employed to let audiences know when it is night.

The Cricket was met at the station by the Wren, who flew him to an inn, bought him a drink, carried his bags upstairs to his room, and was in general so courteous and attentive that the Cricket thought he was the proprietor of the inn.

"I am not a proprietor, but a competitor," the Wren said. "It is a greater honor to be judged by you, even if I should lose, than to win the highest award from a lesser critic and cricket. As small tokens of my esteem, here are a bottle of wine and a cherry pie, and the key to the boudoir of as charming a lady cricket as you would attract in a year of chirping."

That afternoon, the Wren flew the Cricket out to the concert field, where he heard the Frog scrape his cello, the Lark blow his clarion trumpet, the Nightingale strum his lyre of gold, the Blackbird play his boxwood flute, the Catbird run his bright piano arpeggios, and the Partridge show off on his drums. The vocalists came next, beginning with the Canary, a temperamental visitor from abroad, who had sat up all night bragging of his ability and was, as a consequence, in lousy voice. "The Owl can do better than that even if all he can sing is 'Who,'" said the Wren, who had slipped quietly into a chair next to the Cricket's. He gave the critic a cigar, a light, and a swig from a flask. "I shall sing a group of *Lieder*," said the Wren, "all of them Henley's 'Take, Dear, This Little Sheaf of Songs.' I composed the music myself, and dedicated it to my mate and to you."

The Mockingbird sang next, and those in the audience who hoped the amiable Wren would win with his bright little group of songs, all of them the same song, began to worry, for the Mockingbird had slept all night, dreaming of victory, and as a consequence, was in heavenly voice. "I should say his tongue is sharp rather than sweet," whispered the Wren. "When I told him last night that you were a finer fiddler than all the finest fiddlers in the field, he remarked that, to him, you looked like a limousine come to grief at an intersection."

The Cricket rubbed his legs together angrily, producing two low, ominous notes. "In my opinion," the Wren went on, "you look like a shining piece of mechanism, handsome and authoritative, such as the trigger action of a Colt. Here is a lozenge for your cough, and a pillow for your chair, and a footstool for your feet."

When it came time for the Wren to sing, his group of songs, all of them the same song, delighted everybody in the audience except the other soloists and their friends and families.

"I could do better than that," sneered the Mockingbird, "with my beak closed."

"I have thrashed singers with voices ten times better than that," said the Brown Thrasher.

"*Gott im Himmel!*" cried the Canary. "*Er klingt wie ein rostiges eisernes Tor das geölt werden muss.*"

In awarding first prize to the Wren, the Cricket said, in part and in parting, "His voice is like some bright piece of mechanism, such as the works of a golden music box, and he gives his group of one song an infinite variety. This artist also has a keen appreciation of values and a fine critical perception."

In departing, or, to be precise, escaping from, the music festival, the Cricket was fortunate enough to have at his disposal a private airplane, none other than the victorious Wren himself.

MORAL: *It is not always more blessed to give than to receive, but it is frequently more rewarding.*

The Crow
and the Scarecrow

ONCE upon a farm an armada of crows descended like the wolf on the fold. They were after the seeds in the garden and the corn in the field. The crows posted sentinels, who warned them of the approach of the farmer, and they even had an undercover crow or two who mingled with the chickens in the barnyard and the pigeons on the roof, and found out the farmer's plans in advance. Thus they were able to raid the garden and the field when he was away, and they stayed hidden when he was at home. The farmer decided to build a scarecrow so terrifying it would scare the hateful crows to death when they got a good look at it. But the scarecrow, for all the work the farmer put in on it, didn't frighten even the youngest and most fluttery female. The marauders knew that the scarecrow was a suit of old clothes stuffed with straw and that what it held in its wooden hand was not a rifle but only a curtain rod.

As more and more corn and more and more seeds disappeared, the farmer became more and more eager for vengeance. One night, he made himself up to look like a scarecrow and in the dark, for it was a moonless night, his son helped him to take the place of the scarecrow. This time, however, the hand that held the gun was not made of wood and the gun was not an unloaded curtain rod, but a double-barrelled 12-gauge Winchester.

Dawn broke that morning with a sound like a thousand tin pans falling. This was the rebel yell of the crows coming down on field and garden like Jeb Stuart's cavalry. Now one of the young crows who had been out all night, drinking corn instead of eating it, suddenly went into a tailspin, plunged into a bucket of red paint that was standing near the barn, and burst into flames.

The farmer was just about to blaze away at the squadron of crows with both barrels when the one that was on fire headed straight for him. The sight of a red crow, dripping what seemed to be blood, and flaring like a Halloween torch, gave the living scarecrow such a shock that he dropped dead in one beat less than the tick of a watch (which is the way we all want to go, *mutatis*, it need scarcely be said, *mutandis*).

The next Sunday the parson preached a disconsolate sermon, denouncing drink, carryings on, adult delinquency, front page marriages, golf on Sunday, adultery, careless handling of firearms, and cruelty to our feathered friends. After the sermon, the dead farmer's wife explained to the preacher what had really happened, but he only shook his head and murmured skeptically, "Confused indeed would be the time in which the crow scares the scarecrow and becomes the scarescarecrow."

MORAL: *All men kill the thing they hate, too, unless, of course, it kills them first.*

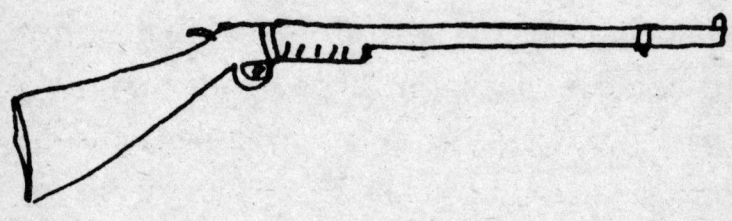

Ivory, Apes, and People

A BAND of ambitious apes in Africa once called upon a herd of elephants with a business proposition. "We can sell your tusks to people for a fortune in peanuts and oranges," said the leader of the apes. "Tusks are tusks to you and us, but to people they are merchandise—billiard balls and piano keys and other things that people buy and sell." The elephants said they would think it over. "Be here tomorrow at this time and we will swing

the deal," said the leader of the apes, and the apes went away to call on some people who were hunting for merchandise in the region.

"It's the very best ivory," the leader of the apes told the leader of the people. "One hundred elephants, two hundred tusks. All yours for oranges and peanuts."

"That's enough ivory for a small ivory tower," said the leader of the people, "or four hundred billiard balls and a thousand piano keys. I will cable my agent to ship your nuts and oranges, and to sell the billiard balls and piano keys. The business of business is business, and the heart of the matter is speed."

"We will close the deal," said the leader of the apes.

"Where is the merchandise now?" inquired the leader of the people.

"It's eating, or mating, but it will be at the appointed place at the appointed hour," replied the chief ape. But it wasn't. The elephants had thought it over, and reconsidered, and they forgot to show up the following day, for elephants are good at forgetting when forgetting is good. There was a great to-do in the marts of world trade when the deal fell through, and everybody, except the elephants, got into the litigation that followed: the Better Business

Bureau, the Monkey Business Bureau, the Interspecies Commerce Commission, the federal courts, the National Association of Merchandisers, the African Bureau of Investigation, the International Association for the Advancement of Animals, and the American Legion. Opinions were handed down, rules were promulgated, subpoenas were issued, injunctions were granted and denied, and objections were sustained and overruled. The Patriotic League of American Women Against Subversion took an active part until it was denounced as subversive by a man who later withdrew his accusation and made a fortune on the sale of two books, "I Made My Bed" and "I Lie in My Teeth."

The elephants kept their ivory, and nobody got any billiard balls or piano keys, or a single nut or an orange.

MORAL: *Men of all degrees should form this prudent habit: never serve a rabbit stew before you catch the rabbit.*

Oliver and the Other Ostriches

AN AUSTERE OSTRICH of awesome authority was lecturing younger ostriches one day on the superiority of their species to all other species. "We were known to the Romans, or, rather, the Romans were known to us," he said. "They called us *avis struthio*, and we called them Romans. The Greeks called us *strouthion*, which means 'truthful one,' or, if it doesn't, it should. We are the biggest birds, and therefore the best."

All his listeners cried, "Hear! Hear!" except a thoughtful one named Oliver. "We can't fly backward like the hummingbird," he said aloud.

"The hummingbird is losing ground," said the old ostrich. "We are going places, we are moving forward."

"Hear! Hear!" cried all the other ostriches except Oliver.

"We lay the biggest eggs and therefore the best eggs," continued the old lecturer.

"The robin's eggs are prettier," said Oliver.

"Robins' eggs produce nothing but robins," said the old ostrich. "Robins are lawn-bound worm addicts."

"Hear! Hear!" cried all the other ostriches except Oliver.

"We get along on four toes, whereas Man needs ten," the elderly instructor reminded his class.

"But Man can fly sitting down, and we can't fly at all," commented Oliver.

The old ostrich glared at him severely, first with one eye and then the other. "Man is flying too fast for a world that is round," he said. "Soon he will catch up with himself, in a great rear-end collision, and Man will never know that what hit Man from behind was Man."

"Hear! Hear!" cried all the other ostriches except Oliver.

"We can make ourselves invisible in time of peril by sticking our heads in the sand," ranted the lecturer. "Nobody else can do that."

"How do we know we can't be seen if we can't see?" demanded Oliver.

"Sophistry!" cried the old ostrich, and all the other ostriches except Oliver cried "Sophistry!" not knowing what it meant.

Just then the master and the class heard a strange alarming sound, a sound like thunder growing close and growing closer. It was not the thunder of weather, though, but the thunder of a vast herd of rogue elephants in full stampede, frightened by nothing, fleeing nowhere. The old ostrich and all the other ostriches except Oliver quickly stuck their heads in the sand. Oliver took refuge behind a large nearby rock until the storm of beasts had passed, and when he came out he beheld a sea of sand and bones and feathers—all that was left of the old teacher and his disciples. Just to be sure, however, Oliver called the roll, but

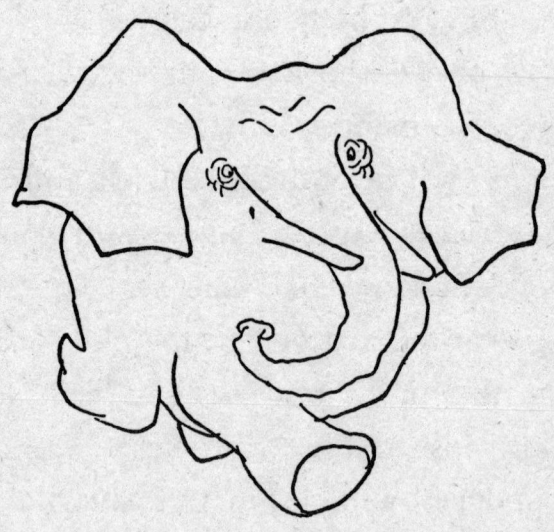

there was no answer until he came to his own name. "Oliver," he said.

"Here! Here!" said Oliver, and that was the only sound there was on the desert except for a faint, final rumble of thunder on the horizon.

MORAL: *Thou shalt not build thy house, nor yet thy faith, upon the sand.*

The Shore
and the Sea

A SINGLE excited lemming started the exodus, crying, "Fire!" and running toward the sea. He may have seen the sunrise through the trees, or waked from a fiery nightmare, or struck his head against a stone, producing stars. Whatever it was, he ran and ran, and as he ran he was joined by others, a mother lemming and her young, a nightwatchlemming on his way home to bed, and assorted revelers and early risers.

"The world is coming to an end!" they shouted, and as the hurrying hundreds turned into thousands, the reasons for their headlong flight increased by leaps and bounds and hops and skips and jumps.

"The devil has come in a red chariot!" cried an elderly male. "The sun is his torch! The world is on fire!"

"It's a pleasure jaunt," squeaked an elderly female.

"A what?" she was asked.

"A treasure hunt!" cried a wild-eyed male who had been up all night. "Full many a gem of purest ray serene the dark unfathomed caves of ocean bear."

"It's a bear!" shouted his daughter. "Go it!" And there were those among the fleeing thousands who shouted "Goats!" and "Ghosts!" until there were almost as many different alarms as there were fugitives.

One male lemming who had lived alone for many years refused to be drawn into the stampede that swept past his cave like a flood. He saw no flames in the forest, and no devil, or bear, or goat, or ghost. He had long ago decided, since he was a serious scholar, that the caves of ocean bear no gems, but only soggy glub and great gobs of mucky gump. And so he watched the other lemmings leap into the sea and disappear beneath the waves, some crying "We are saved!" and some crying "We are lost!" The scholarly lemming shook his head sorrowfully, tore up what he had written through the years about his species, and started his studies all over again.

MORAL: *All men should strive to learn before they die what they are running from, and to, and why.*